THE MALVERN HILLS

THE MALVERN HILLS

TRAVELS THROUGH ELGAR COUNTRY · ARCHIE MILES

FOREWORD BY

SIR DAVID WILLCOCKS

PAVILION

For Jan, my love and inspiration

First published in Great Britain in 1992 by
PAVILION BOOKS LIMITED
196 Shaftesbury Avenue, London WC2H 8JL

Designed by Andrew Barron & Collis Clements Associates

A CIP record for this book is available from the British Library.

ISBN 1 85145 731 3 (Hb)
ISBN 1 85145 868 9 (Pb)
10 9 8 7 6 5 4 3 2 1

Typeset by Bookworm Typesetting, Manchester
Printed and bound in Portugal by Printer Portuguesa

Page 1: Sunrise along the Malvern Hills from Broad Down

Page 3: Early morning jogger heads into the mists from Worcestershire Beacon

Herefordshire lit up for a new day

CONTENTS

I will lift up mine eyes unto the hills: from whence cometh my help.

THOSE WORDS FROM Psalm 121 have for centuries brought comfort and reassurance to countless men and women in public worship and in private devotions. As a boy chorister in the choir of Westminster Abbey I probably sang the psalm forty or fifty times, always conjuring up the vision of a beautiful range of hills, timeless and serene, far removed from the busy city in which I lived. I remember trying to reflect calm confidence in my singing of that verse.

It was with dismay that some years later I learnt that the Psalmist's hills, far from being serene, were the abode of robbers; furthermore 'from whence cometh my help' was not a statement of fact, but an anxious question to which the answer was revealed in the next verse, 'My help cometh even from the Lord'.

Be that as it may, the vision of my childhood has prevailed throughout my life; mountains and hills have been for me symbols of strength and stability, silent signposts to the sky.

Amongst many memories of my childhood is the occasion when Sir Edward Elgar, in court dress as Master of the King's Musick, conducted the choirs of Westminster Abbey and the Chapel Royal at the unveiling of a statue to Queen Alexandra: it was for me the beginning of a lifelong love of his music. I little thought that some twenty years later I would be appointed Organist and Master of the Choristers at Worcester Cathedral in succession to Sir Ivor Atkins who had been one of Elgar's closest friends; still less that I would have the joy of conducting many of the composer's greatest choral and orchestral works in the Cathedral that he loved.

With that experience it was understandable that I should feel a strong urge to visit the cottage where Elgar was born and the places where he later lived and worked; to walk on the Malvern Hills; and to explore the countryside from which the composer avowedly derived inspiration. I soon reckoned that I knew the area well and that I had experienced in ample measure the beauty of the Malvern Hills.

A study of the wonderful collection of photographs by Archie Miles contained in this book makes me realise, years later, how much I missed on my walks, enjoyable as they

M*orning burns bright on Castlemorton Common*

were. Only an artist with the patience of Archie Miles would be prepared to wait on the hills for days or maybe weeks to capture the lifting of the blue-grey mist at dawn, the angry black clouds heralding a violent storm at midday, and the sky ablaze with myriad hues at sunset. Only an artist with his eye for detail would look out for unusual cloud formations, reflections in water, and the subtle interplay of light and shade. Only an artist with his sensitivity would be able to convey in pictorial form the stillness, the silence and the solitariness that Elgar expressed so imaginatively in music at the beginning of Part II of *The Dream of Gerontius*.

The photographs in this book will undoubtedly evoke personal memories. I cannot look at the poppy on page 60 and read of Elgar's depression on account of the horror of World War I without remembering the officers and other ranks of the 1st Battalion of the Worcestershire Regiment who were killed in Normandy during World War II, for many of those young men were born and lived within sight of the Malvern Hills.

I hope that many people will derive as much joy as I already have from this book and that some may wish to follow in the footsteps of Archie Miles and experience more fully the beauties of the Malvern Hills.

Ancient oak on earthworks near Whiteleaved Oak

The mountains also shall bring peace: and the little hills righteousness unto the people.
(Psalm 72)

David Willcocks

ACKNOWLEDGEMENTS

James Bennett, curator of the Elgar Birthplace Trust;
John McGregor at Malvern Priory;
Michael Kennedy *'Portrait of Elgar'*
Michael Grundy *'Elgar's Beloved Country'*
Pamela Hurle *'Portrait of Malvern'* and *Bygone Malvern'*
Mr Peters of Birts Street;
Brian Seed for his guidance in the early years;
Bill Taylor of Winchcombe;
Julie Davis, my editor;
Colin Webb for his faith and vision;
and last, but by no means least
the music of Sir Edward Elgar

SURVEYED ACROSS THE Worcestershire plain, the sleeping beast that is the Malvern Hills lies bathed in an early morning glow. It is these hills that quietly witness my entry into Elgar Country, by way of Upton upon Severn, and will watch over my progress through their domain. This was a landscape so beloved by Edward Elgar that he returned constantly to his old haunts throughout his life. This was the country which stirred the spirit within the man. For Elgar the purest expression of his love for this homeland was through his music. To listen is to sense the powerful surge of emotion from a man uniquely charged by the beauty of his world. As a photographer I have not attempted to map out the finest details of Elgar's life, homes, work places, and so on, but to seek the essence of the landscape which fired the composer's inspiration.

I have taken Elgar's love of his native rivers as my first theme, and followed the broad course of the River Severn northward through Kempsey, where he lived for several years during the 1920s, to the city of Worcester. The city that was so pivotal throughout Elgar's life has changed somewhat since his day. Now it is a vigorous city, sharply attuned to the nineties, and one of the few oases from the hustle and bustle is the cathedral. The boy Elgar was often in or around the building, listening and learning; later the accomplished composer had most of his works performed within the cathedral – most notably *The Dream of Gerontius*, which had its triumphal first British performance there. It is fitting, therefore, that the Elgar Memorial Window depicts *The Dream of Gerontius*.

A few miles to the west of Worcester lies the little village of Lower Broadheath. Here, on 2 June 1857, Edward Elgar was born in the tiny brick cottage that has now become the Birthplace Museum; a small yet cherished shrine to the great composer. Further west lies the Teme valley, which was a continual source of delight to Elgar. There is one particular stretch of the river near Knightwick that was Elgar's most idyllic spot. The exact location is unknown, for he shared it with only the closest of friends. Unlike the broad and steady flow of the Severn, as it passes through Worcestershire, the Teme is a river of twists and turns, of deep valleys and different moods – sometimes sluggish and glassy, sometimes breaking into a boisterous rush of white water. Little has changed in the last century in the Teme valley, where peace and tranquility still reign supreme.

A little distance to the south, between the Teme and the Malvern Hills, lies 'Birchwood'; the cottage at Storridge which the Elgars rented as a summer house between

1898 and 1903. Here, in this rural retreat, Elgar was in his element, and the creative juices flowed freely. Most notable was his completion of *The Dream of Gerontius* on 3 August 1900. During this period of his life Elgar achieved the summit of his creativity, scoring such masterpieces as the *Enigma* Variations, in 1899, and *Pomp and Circumstance March No. 1*, in 1901. While at 'Birchwood' he took to riding a bicycle and made many excursions about the countryside, where he was often overtaken by musical inspiration.

This leads into my second theme: the essence of the country and its villages, through which Elgar would roam in search of spiritual refreshment and inspiration. From the bumps and tumbles of Suckley Hills, I follow his wanderings across to the deliciously named Golden Valley, and down the west side of the Malvern Hills, through the villages of Cradley and Mathon to Ledbury; all the while the temptation of the Malvern range beckoning beyond. Then, having teased myself enough, I relent and head for the Malvern Hills, leaving behind the rolling woodland and meadows of Herefordshire, skip across the hills at Wynd's Point, where once lived Jenny Lind ('The Swedish Nightingale'), and descend into Great Malvern, where the Elgars made their home between 1891 and 1904. This delightful spa town has a rich inheritance of Victorian architecture, dating from its heyday in the 1860s, through a period of increasing expansion and popularity, up to the turn of the century. The whole town, clinging, sometimes precariously, to the eastern slopes of the Malvern Hills, is superbly offset by the splendour of Malvern Priory, with its wealth of medieval glass, tiles and wood carving. The town of Great Malvern, together with its smaller family members of Little Malvern, Malvern Wells and West Malvern, take a great pride in their heritage. Streets are clean, parks are manicured to perfection, and the buildings are beautifully preserved and, through the summer months, adorned with flowers. Remarkable features like the glorious railway station and the fully functional Victorian gas lamps keep the original spirit of the Victorian spa much in evidence.

The Malvern Hills seem to watch over the town tucked beneath their slopes, but beyond the houses those slopes of continually changing colours rise steeply away to the summit of Worcestershire Beacon, at 1,395 feet the highest hill in the Malvern range. Here I embark on the third main theme of this journey through Elgar Country. For the wanderer in this landscape the Malvern Hills are omnipresent. The dominating feature of the area, they create high drama, while at the same time exuding a great benevolence. Even though the hills are not particularly high, they still foster that elation one experiences in high places, looking down on the rest of the world. To stride the ridge along the old boundary between Worcestershire and Herefordshire is to take in a dramatic dichotomy between the flat expanse of the Worcestershire plain, as it sprawls across to the Cotswolds, and the humps and bumps of Herefordshire rolling away to the Welsh mountains. For me, the best times to be on these heights are at dawn and dusk. The peace, the solitude and the wondrous quality of light give me the kind of natural euphoria that must surely be akin to those moments from which Elgar drew his own inspiration. The Malvern Hills were the epicentre of Elgar's being, from the fire of his boyhood bareback horse rides across the tops to the embers of his final days in Worcester, from where he would gaze at his beloved hills.

Worcestershire Beacon may offer the most exciting viewpoint, but the most striking hill along the Malvern range has been moulded by the hand of man. Herefordshire Beacon, otherwise known as British Camp, is an Iron Age hill fort, whose ancient defences were to inspire Elgar to write *Caractacus*. Popular legend relates how from this earthwork the great chieftain of the Britons made his last defiant stand against the might of the Roman armies. This has now been disproved by historians, but on a stormy winter's day or beneath a thunderous summer sky it all seems eminently believable. Southward, beyond British Camp, the Malvern Hills enter a kind of twilight zone. Midsummer Hill, Chase End Hill and the settlements of Hollybush and Whiteleaved Oak are composed of homesteads tucked into the nooks and crannies of the hills, amongst the bracken and the woodland which bursts with bluebells each spring.

This atmosphere of independence, of solitude, and of a land lost in time pervades eastward over Castlemorton Common and on to Longdon Marsh. Far across the Marsh, most of which has now been tamed by agriculture, run long skeins of aged willows which bend and thrash in the teeth of gales, stormy rain and blizzards. From this wilderness came the inspiration for *The Apostles*. A short way off lies Upton upon Severn, and the journey ends as it began. The bridge that spans the river is a gateway, a crossing over, the symbol of my humble attempt to enter Elgar Country, to understand his vision and inspiration, which I offer in the light of my own journey.

Archie Miles
February 1991

The gazer stares at water glass
That smoulders in the first born rays
Silent inward joy fullblown
Seeing the unseen rise from haze

*Every day brings a new dawn
and paints a different picture.*

Daybreak in Elgar Country. The sun rises across the River Severn above Upton.

The prospect westward from Longdon Hill End, with the distinctive shapes of the Malvern Hills bathed in winter sun.

A *dragonfly alights briefly on a buttercup in water meadows beside the Severn.*

A *timber-framed cottage nestles snugly into the landscape at Hanley Castle.*

Survivor of the fury, a beech tree on Old Hills with the Malvern Hills beyond bathed in early sunlight.

Lazily snorting and munching their way beneath the oak canopy, cattle graze in the early morning rays.

Come you to this place and dream awhile
For far along the river mirrored sky
Draws thoughts unspoken from a private smile
Known only by the few with hearts to fly

Men who angle hard by on the bend
Will wonder at the tranquil dawning day
And warmed by willow filtered rays again
Hopeful cast their lot within and pray

Lift me up and carry me downstream
Down along the drowsy meadows where
The early mist clad cattle snort and steam
As bees fly out to sample floral fare

*Early morning sun steals across
the Severn from behind St Mary's
church Kempsey.*

A *tantalizing glimpse of Worcestershire Beacon through the towering yews in the churchyard of St Mary's, Kempsey.*

S*wans glide majestically up the river Severn below Kempsey; a scene once familiar to Elgar when he lived at Napleton Grange between 1923 and 1927.*

The village pond was once a feature of most English villages, but sadly few have survived. This beautifully preserved example, complete with ducks and water lilies, is in the aptly named village of Hanley Swan.

The churchyard at Claines, to the north of Worcester, where the teenage Elgar sat by the graves of his maternal grandparents to study scores by the great composers.

On 2 June 1857 Edward William Elgar was born in this modest little house in Lower Broadheath, to the west of Worcester. It is now a museum, a veritable shrine to Elgar, housing many treasures associated with the composer's life.

As the thunderous storm clouds roll in from the north-west, the low afternoon sun vividly illuminates the birthplace for a brief exciting moment.

The Elgar Memorial Window in the north aisle of Worcester Cathedral, depicting The Dream of Gerontius.

Hop kilns at Doddenham.

A hop yard at Knightwick, its vast network of wires reminiscent of some giant rural terminus waiting for its trams to arrive.

Reflections along the Teme, near Darbys Green, with the early sun glinting through the alders.

Early morning view up the River Teme between Bransford Court and Dawshill.

Windfall crab-apples among
tree roots at Brockamin.

Morning sunshine floods over
The Lodge at Laughern Hill.

His own precious place lies near
Little changed to all who pass
Soft willows silver swishing fear
Not their imminent crack demise

Mirror trees ripple softly green
While just beyond the silence
Rushes running water fast unseen
Until once more the peace descends

*Fishermen bide their time in the
late afternoon on a sharp bend in
the Teme near Broadwas Court.*

A *storm-blasted willow by the Teme above Whitbourne.*

T*he vivid greens of May along the banks of the Teme near Whitbourne.*

In the deeps beyond the reeds lies another world.

View up the Teme towards Whitbourne Ford from below Ankerdine Hill.

A *much leant-on and rather forlorn cast-iron hound on one of the Victorian benches in the churchyard of St Peter's, Martley.*

A *thirteenth-century wall painting in the chancel, which depicts a hart representing Christ. St Peter's has many remarkable wall paintings of mythical beasts and geometric patterns.*

The shadows stretch across the pastures on Ridge Hill as a peaceful July evening draws to a close above the Teme valley.

The late sun of a summer evening filters across the Teme valley north of Shelsley Beauchamp.

Aqueous gems clad this early morning cobweb on the slopes of the Teme valley below Ham Bridge.

The glass breaks into laughter at a bend in the River Teme near Martley.

'Desirable black and white timber-framed property' at Riley Cottage, near Oxhall, above the Teme valley.

Built at the end of the fourteenth century, the Manor House at Lower Brockhampton epitomizes the timber-framed style of architecture so closely associated with Herefordshire.

'The sound is like the rushing of the wind – the summer wind among the lofty pines' – Elgar.

Sunrise through a clump of pine trees behind 'Birchwood', at Storridge, the house where Elgar completed The Dream of Gerontius on 3 August 1900.

Long shadows of early morning reach across the pasture behind 'Birchwood', while beyond lie the Malvern Hills – a view which Elgar loved.

There are many hidden dwellers in the woodland.

In the springtime the bright shining faces of primroses adorn the hedgerows and woodlands.

Hidden away in the woodland beneath Old Storridge Common, the Leigh Brook gently trickles down into the Teme valley.

The first fallen alder leaves of autumn cling to a boulder in the Leigh Brook.

Adam and Eve being cast out of the Garden of Eden – seventeenth-century Flemish glass in Alfrick church.

The cries of swifts break the summer morning peace as they wheel around the church of St Mary Magdalene at Alfrick. The unusual tower, recently restored, is clad in shingles. Also remarkable is the large sundial, given by the local Allies family, and bearing the words: 'On this moment hangs eternity'.

Lewis Carroll's brother was once the curate here, and Carroll often stayed with him at the rectory.

One of Elgar's most renowned compositions, the Pomp and Circumstance March No. 1, became the setting for "Land of Hope and Glory". The song mirrored the patriotic fervour associated with the onset of the Great War, but Elgar disliked its jingoism from the start, and became deeply depressed by the horror of the conflict.

Evening sunlight washes over an old wall at Alfrick Court.

Poplars and conifers form a wind-break around a vineyard near Suckley, while the tower of St John the Baptist peeps through the trees.

Early morning view northward to Old Storridge Common from West Malvern.

*A*n ivy-clad barn roof at Lower Court in Suckley.

*E*vening view up to Bearswood Common from Batchelor's Bridge, near Suckley.

Hops growing in profusion at Paunton Court in The Golden Valley. Traditionally hops are associated with the brewing of beer, but herbal pillows stuffed with hops are reputed to aid sleep and relieve tension. The bitter-sweet aroma of the hops at harvest time is never forgotten.

The lush green landscape exudes its summer scents from rain-soaked foliage as the storm-clouds roll away and the low evening sun floods the folds of Herefordshire from Fox Hill to the Malverns.

An exhilarating cloudscape scuds across Golden Valley, north of Bishop's Frome.

The view westward across the Golden Valley at Paunton Court, near Acton Beauchamp. One of those blustery days when little snatches of sunlight worry the landscape.

The hedgerows of April glow white with the blossom of damson trees. Once the fruit was harvested and sold to the textile industry for use as a dye, but with the advent of synthetic dyes the fruit is now the preserve of the jam and winemakers.

Late evening view down the Lodon valley across typical rolling country of Herefordshire to the distant Malvern Hills

E*arly morning view westward through a gap in the oaks at Halesend.*

A *rainbow arcs over Bearswood Common and Halesend Wood as the last day of October brings stormy weather beating down across Greenhill.*

A *detail of the fifteenth-century parish hall at Cradley, which was once the village Grammar School.*

T*he last sun of a glorious June day glances across Church Cottage in Cradley.*

Shadows now cast long upon the ground
The embers of a fullblown June day glow
While softly from within the organ's sound
Regales each swift and swallow swooping low

Stone memories have gathered warmth all day
The lichen crusted dear departed slept
Down deep within the body of yew lay
The spirit of this place forever kept

*The heart of an ancient yew tree
in Cradley churchyard.*

Morning haze rolls back from
Coddington as the first rays of a
new day reach over Coombe Hill.

Below Coddington at the day's
end, rolls of hay lie scattered
across the fields like pieces of
some giant game.

A promising morning dips into a grey day on the hills above Petty France. The distinctive shape of the hill fort of British Camp can be seen in the distance.

Early morning through the trees to Oyster Hill, beyond which lies Hope End, once the family home of Elizabeth Barrett Browning.

I remember spotting it from a distance
And how happy it made me feel
In a landscape patchwork
So often glowing yellow
With that musty scented rape
This was different
Some farmer
Whether by desire or no
Left his hillside untroubled
To grow golden yellow with buttercups

Enough no doubt to discover
Whether the whole of Hereford and Worcester
Like butter

*A vast buttercup meadow near
Mathon Court.*

A *diffused grey morning creeps gently over the Malvern Hills, viewed from the hills near Hope End.*

H*erefordshire Beacon, wrapped in early mists, seen from near Old Colwall.*

Cattle at Bank Farm near West Malvern.

The sun dips down beyond Ledbury, leaving behind it a trail of swirls and whisps.

A *foggy morning begins to clear near Kilbury Camp.*

T*he quaint delight of Eastnor post office, which was once the village forge.*

Let me take you on a journey
Through a dream that I once flew
Over mountains under curtains
Down a moonlit avenue

Where the faces rarely seen
Watched from narrow lidded eyes
Of the homes upon the hillside
In their deck-like alibis

How the stars bejewel this mantle
Over plain disected by
Teaming waters seventh heaven
Blended at the battle cry

Sense the pulse that flutters softly
In the beast that lies asleep
For she has borne those Britons bravely
Beckoned by their hilltop keep

*M*orning sparkles in Upper
Wyche.

Part of the splendid display at Baskerville House, in Upper Wyche, Malvern, a short walk away from 'Craeg Lea', where the Elgars lived for five years at the turn of the century.

One of Malvern's oldest shops is that of Cridlan & Walker, butchers and fruit and vegetable merchants. The striking Gothic frontage, which has been preserved in its original form throughout its 150-year existence, makes a perfect foil for the adjoining Abbey gateway and the Priory beyond.

Malvern Priory is thought to house the best collection of medieval wall tiles in the country. Dating from the latter half of the fifteenth century, they were made in kilns close by the Priory. There are nearly one hundred different designs, inlaid rather than merely painted, and remarkable for their artistry and quality.

Malvern Priory by night.

Designed by local architect E.W. Elmslie and built in 1861, Great Malvern is one of the finest station buildings in the land. Recently restored to its Victorian splendour, its colourful ironwork is at its most decorative in the variety of floral capitals.

The bandstand in Priory Park.

St Ann's Well above Great Malvern is dedicated to the patron saint of springs. Here the water is remarkable for its purity rather than any particular mineral content. Victorians in droves climbed the steep hillside from the hotels and hydropathic establishments to 'take the cure'.

On a tablet above the well:

Drink of this crystal fountain
And praise the loving Lord
Who from the rocky mountain
This living stream out-poured
Fit emblem of the holy fount
That flows from God's eternal mount

One of three particularly early pillar boxes located in Malvern. They were cast in Birmingham in 1857 – the year of Elgar's birth.

I will follow you wherever you may go
And love you through our time however long
To nestle always to your breast and grow
Still closer in the flow of love's sweet song

View north from Worcestershire Beacon to North Hill as the low morning light picks out the contours.

Hand in hand down from Worcestershire Beacon into the morning mist.

At the end of a bright November day the sun slips away from North Hill and the houses of West Malvern which cling to the steep slopes.

Early morning mists shroud the land below the western slopes of the Malvern Hills, viewed from Worcestershire Beacon.

The sort of day when vicious winds lash the tops and rain drives down like stair rods. The sun bursts through briefly and illuminates the vista to the south-west of Worcestershire Beacon.

Late summer sun catches the Malvern Hills as they stretch southward from Worcestershire Beacon.

*S*torm clouds rumble towards
Worcestershire Beacon from the
west.

*W*inter skeletons of silver
birches on the eastern slopes of
Worcestershire Beacon.

Larch woodland on the western slopes of the Malvern Hills above Colwall Stone.

'This is what I hear all day – the trees are singing my music – or have I sung theirs?' – Elgar

Autumnal bramble and rowan leaves on silver birch bark.

Midsummer morning
northward along the Malvern
Hills with clouds skidding across
the summit of Worcestershire
Beacon.

The same view, but on a crisp
November morning.

This is the twilight time
When once the lamplighter trod his measured way
From post to post across his spa town beat
To catch the gas and break the gloom
A haven beacon shines from every case
Magnetic to the moths on summer wing
A pony chaise trips by to bring the lady home
This balmy summer eve
While down the lane full to the brim
With twopenny nutbrown cheer
Well met fellows roll home to bed
And sweet oblivion

Evening breezes rustle the leaves around one of Malvern's Victorian gas lamps, on the road down to Mathon Lodge. About a hundred of these lamps survive in working order, and are located in various parts of Malvern.

An Edwardian letterbox with its stone surround seemingly propping up a barn at Brand Green.

View down the eastern slopes of Herefordshire Beacon to Little Malvern Priory and the edge of the autumn world.

The windflower, or wood anemone. Alice Stuart-Wortley, the daughter of the painter John Everitt Millais, was to become a dear friend of the Elgars, and is reputed to have been the inspiration for Elgar's Violin Concerto. Edward gave her the affectionate name of 'Windflower' because he felt that Alice's grace and beauty were epitomized by the pale nodding flowers.

Shafts of early sunlight pierce the clouds over the Worcestershire plain.

A *weather-vane at Chesham Cottage above Brand Green.*

M*ay-time view north-west from the Malvern Hills above Colwall Stone.*

A dramatic sunset over Colwall.

Early morning view along the western edge of the Malvern Hills.

Hand rest on the medieval monks' stalls in Little Malvern Priory. Two little pigs with their heads buried in a trough.

A gap in the trees reveals Little Malvern Priory and Little Malvern Court nestling below the eastern slopes of the Malvern Hills, while beyond, in the middle distance, lies the village of Welland.

The view north from British Camp when November snow has hung its chilly coat across the Malvern Hills.

A winter guardian watches over Longdon Marsh through the biting winds of February. While out on Longdon Marsh Elgar was inspired to write The Apostles.

A *hot humid afternoon on the eastern slopes of the Malvern Hills, but in the cool woodland depths a gentle breeze stirs the emerald bracked fronds.*

S*unrise at Broad Down below British Camp.*

I've strode this ridge for years
Braced I waited on this windswept edge
So often the gales ripped through the thorn
Still May bears witness to the bridal bloom
No passer-by will care to see me here
Come winter blast and birds will pluck the prize
My ever changing filigree will grace this skyline
Through deep-rooted faith in the four winds
I will survive

A *morning scene across the*
Worcestershire plain from
Hangman's Hill.

131

The tramp of many feet packs an icy path up to the Iron Age hill fort of British Camp, otherwise known as Herefordshire Beacon. It was this ancient fortress which inspired Elgar to write Caractacus, as it was once believed that Caractacus had made his last stand against the might of the Roman armies from this vantage point.

A wintry morning view, west of British Camp, seen across Netherton Farm.

Blue euphoria
More wondrous with every step
All consuming scent
Entices deeper bluer yet

The soft shades of the bluebell carpet beneath the trees on the eastern slopes of Midsummer Hill.

The fresh new foliage of a mature beech glows in the early sunlight on Midsummer Hill.

Sunrise across the bluebells on Midsummer Hill.

Sheep trudge through the February snow in search of food, near Hollybush, with Hollybed Common beyond.

Misty morning southward from the Hill Fort at Midsummer Hill.

The people lie snug asleep
The dreams pass away
The mist clears
The day stirs
The sun red rises
The trees whisper to each other
The earth takes warmth and stretches
The awakening

The rosy pink balloon of a new
day floats up across
Worcestershire, viewed from
Midsummer Hill.

*S*un breaks through a sweet
chestnut in The Gullett.

A tiny pond on Castlemorton
Common, surrounded by
pollarded willows.

The view north from Hollybush, where the land sweeps gracefully up from the Worcestershire plain on to the Malvern Hills in midwinter . . .

. . . and high summer

Duck on a blue skied lake in Golden Valley, near Hollybush.

The last rays of the day glance across Chase End Hill. In the distance lies the western escarpment of the Cotswolds.

A *huge knot of mistletoe enmeshed within the boughs of an old cider apple tree. Once mistletoe was relatively common throughout England, but now it is almost totally confined to the Worcester and Hereford area.*

B *eneath the rushing storm-clouds the low light of autumn imparts an iridescence to Golden Valley and the Malvern Hills beyond.*

A shaft of sunlight catches the effigy of William Caldwell, Rear-Admiral of the Royal Navy's Baltic fleet (died 1718), reclining on his grandiose tomb in Birtsmorton church.

At 8 a.m. Mr Peters takes in his milk at 'Providence Bungalow' in Birts Street. The cottage was once a carriage belonging to the Midland Railway.

151

Bill *Taylor of Winchcombe thatching a cottage near Upton upon Severn.*

Not *only does 'the Haven' at Wayend Street boast a superb thatched roof, but also thatched dovecots in the garden!*

Erected during the Great War
the corrugated vernacular of
Hollybush Church Room stands
resplendent by the roadside in a
fresh coat of paint.

Resembling a child's toy fort
with its large round corner
turrets, Eastnor Castle lies
between the Malvern Hills and
Ledbury. Built in 1812 the Castle
was designed by Sir Robert
Smirke who also built the British
Museum.

The end of the day across the river at Upton upon Severn. Behind the welcoming glow of the Plough Inn looms the tower of the old church of 1769, affectionately known to the locals as the 'Pepper Pot'.

Another wondrous morning launches the new day across the river at Upton.

INDEX